RUNNING

FOR FUN!

By Jessica Deutsch

Content Adviser: Charlie Mahler, Runner, Coach, and Freelance Writer, Northfield, Minnesota
Reading Adviser: Frances J. Bonacci, Ed.D., Reading Specialist, Cambridge, Massachusetts

Compass Point Books ◆ Minneapolis, Minnesota

Compass Point Books
3109 West 50th Street, #115
Minneapolis, MN 55410

This book was manufactured with paper containing
at least 10 percent post-consumer waste.

Photographs ©: Stephen Coburn/Shutterstock, cover (left), 13 (bottom), 14 (bottom); Alexander Kalina/Shutterstock, cover (right), back cover;
Private Collection/The Bridgeman Art Library, 4; photobar/Shutterstock, 5; Loris Eichenberger/Shutterstock, 6; Radius Images/Jupiter Images, 9 (front);
photobank.ch/Shutterstock, 9 (back); David Davis/BigStockPhoto, 10; Ingram Publishing/Jupiter Images, 11, 47; Joe Brandt/iStockphoto, 12; Franck
Camhi/iStockphoto, 13 (top); Reuben Schulz/iStockphoto, 13 (middle); Stephen Morris/iStockphoto, 14 (top); Rex USA, 15; Frances L Fruit/Shutterstock,
16; TriggerPhoto/iStockphoto, 17; AP Images/Andy King, 19 (front); Tor Lindqvist/iStockphoto, 19 (back); George Clerk/iStockphoto, 20–21; Kris Butler/
Shutterstock, 23; Kovalev Serguei/Shutterstock, 25; Galina Barskaya/Shutterstock, 26–27; Jaimie Duplass/Shutterstock, 28; Alex Brosa/iStockphoto,
29; Image Source Pink/Jupiter Images, 30; AlexFox/iStockphoto, 31; Carsten Medom Madsen/Shutterstock, 32 (front); AP Images/Will Powers, 32–33;
Cameron Cross/Shutterstock, 34; AP Images/Nora Gruner, 35; Larry St. Pierre/Shutterstock, 36; Bill Grove/iStockphoto, 37; Eric Feferberg/AFP/Getty
Images, 38; Library of Congress, 39; Norman Potter/Central Press/Getty Images, 40–41; Tony Duffy/Allsport/Getty Images, 41 (front), 43 (middle); North
Wind Picture Archives, 42 (left); Private Collection/The Stapleton Collection/The Bridgeman Art Library, 42 (right); AP Images, 43 (left); Jamie McDonald/
Getty Images, 43 (right); Sebastien Windal/Shutterstock, 44 (left); Spencer Platt/Getty Images, 44 (right); AP Images/Kevin Wolf, 45.

Editor: Brenda Haugen
Page Production: Ashlee Schultz
Photo Researcher: Eric Gohl
Creative Director: Keith Griffin
Editorial Director: Nick Healy
Managing Editor: Catherine Neitge

Library of Congress Cataloging-in-Publication Data
Deutsch, Jessica.
  Running for fun! / by Jessica Deutsch.
      p. cm. — (For fun!)
  Includes index.
  ISBN 978-0-7565-3629-9 (library binding)
  1. Running—Juvenile literature. I. Title. II. Series.
  GV1061.D48 2008
  796.42—dc22   2007038687

Visit Compass Point Books on the Internet at www.compasspointbooks.com
or e-mail your request to custserv@compasspointbooks.com

Table of Contents

Note: In this book, there are two kinds of vocabulary words. Running Words to Know are words specific to running. They are defined on page 46. Other Words to Know are helpful words that aren't related only to running. They are defined on page 47.

Running for Everyone

People have competed in running races for centuries. The sport's history in the Olympics began before 776 B.C. Today running is one of the most popular sports. People all over the world run on a regular basis. Even if you are not an Olympian or a competitive athlete, running can become a fun part of your life.

Many people think running is a grueling sport. But what they don't know is that running gets easier if you take some time to learn how to run.

Do you remember the first running step you took? Not many people do. Running is one of the most natural activities for us. We learn it so early in life that most of us probably don't remember running for the first time. Often we don't take the time to think how we can do it better. But with just a little guidance, anyone can master the techniques that make running easy—and fun!

If you look around, you will probably see people running in many ways. Some run in groups, while others prefer to run alone. Some run on machines called treadmills, while others run on tracks, trails, or roads. Some people only like to jog, while others like to run fast. You should think about what would be most fun for you.

Really Fast Fact

Did you know that some of the best runners in the world are not humans but animals? The cheetah is a sprinter that can reach high speeds to catch its prey. And the antelope has been known to cover long distances at up to 61 miles (98 kilometers) per hour! An antelope will outrun almost any animal that chases it.

Getting on Track

An official outdoor track is a flat, oval surface that is usually divided into eight or nine lanes. Modern tracks are made from rubber. They measure 400 meters around the first lane.

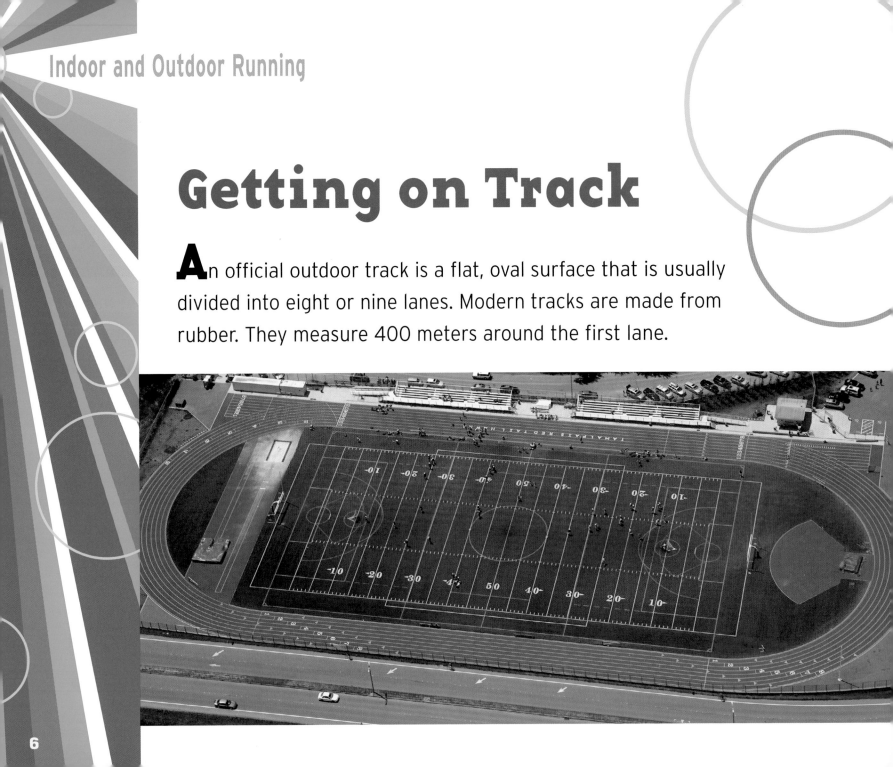

Indoor tracks are most useful in areas with cold, snowy winters. Most indoor tracks are 200 meters around and have six lanes.

All track meets score runners based on how they place in their events. For example, a runner winning an event earns more points than the runner who finishes in second place. A team's score is the sum of all its members' points. The team with the highest score wins the meet.

Racing Distances

In the United States, English units of measurement—inches, feet, yards, and miles—are most commonly used in everyday life. However, most other countries have adopted the metric system of measurement. Most tracks today are measured in meters, a unit of measurement in the metric system.

Some common outdoor race distances in meters, miles, and laps are:

100 meters = 1 straightaway on the track
200 meters = about ⅛ mile = ½ lap
400 meters = about ¼ mile = 1 lap, also called a quarter
800 meters = about ½ mile = 2 laps
1,500 meters = 3¾ laps
1,600 meters = 4 laps
1 mile = 1,609 meters, or just over 4 laps
3,000 meters = 1.864 miles = 7½ laps
5,000 meters = 3.1 miles = 12½ laps
8,000 meters = 4.97 miles
10,000 meters = 6.2 miles

Hitting the Trails

If you love nature, cross country is a great way to enjoy the outdoors and practice running. Cross country refers to running on off-road trails or grass surfaces. Park trails that are well-maintained and well-marked are popular with cross-country runners.

Unlike track running, cross-country running can vary greatly in difficulty. Some routes are hilly, while others are flat. Some have a rough terrain. The best way to find out what a trail is like is to ask another runner who knows the area well. You also may be able to find information on the Internet. Many parks have trail descriptions online or in brochures at their offices.

The Paved Path

Road running is often the easiest, most convenient way to run. You can run almost anywhere: Just step out your front door, and you're at your starting line! Road running refers to running on pavement or concrete surfaces that pedestrians and bikers use. Road running is much like cross-country running; the difficulty of your run depends on where you live. The terrain can be hilly or flat.

Usually it is not safe to run on roads used by cars. The only time it is safe is during road races when the streets have been closed to vehicles. These road races are managed by police and race officials to make sure that cars stay off the course. If you are not in a road race, stick to sidewalks and pedestrian paths for running, and be sure to use crosswalks.

Road racing happens all year, although the spring, summer, and fall are especially popular racing seasons. Races of a variety of distances take place on roads and streets, around lakes, along rivers and seas, and through neighborhoods.

Lacing Up

Running is simple and inexpensive. Runners don't need a lot of equipment to get started, but one item can't be forgotten: running shoes.

Running shoes: Shoes with enough cushion and support help relieve the impact the body experiences during running. Good running shoes provide traction so you don't slip. Your shoes should be replaced regularly—either every six months or every 350 to 500 miles (563 to 804 kilometers) you run, whichever comes first.

Sunscreen: To protect your skin from the sun, use a sunscreen with an SPF of 30 or higher.

Clothing: If you are running outside, dress for the weather. In hot weather, light clothing is the best choice. Light clothing "breathes," which means it allows the moisture from sweat to evaporate so that the body can cool itself. When it is cold outside, be sure to wear layers and winter gear such as a hat and gloves. Reflective patches on your clothing or shoes make you more visible early in the morning, at dusk, and in the dark.

Water bottle: Having water handy during and after a run is important. You need to replace the fluids your body loses when you sweat.

More Gear

Chronograph: A special running watch called a chronograph has a timing function that will help you keep track of how long you have been running.

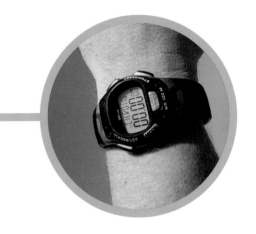

Treadmill: A treadmill is a machine with a moving surface that allows you to run in one place. Treadmills are useful during bad weather conditions and are available at many gyms and recreation centers.

Racing spikes and flats: These are special lightweight shoes often used during races. Spikes have less cushion than training shoes and are made of lightweight materials. They also have four to eight holes where small, screwlike spikes can be attached to the shoe with a spike wrench. Spikes vary in length from 1/16 to 1/4 inch (0.4 to 0.6 centimeters). Spikes provide extra traction and are often used for track races or cross-country races when the terrain is slippery. When traction isn't a problem, runners sometimes choose flats instead of spikes. Flats are lighter than training shoes.

Take It Easy

At first, running can seem very hard. If you're excited to get started, you might want to dive in and do it all. But this might leave you tired, sore, and frustrated. Don't make this mistake!

As a beginner, patience is important. Ease into running. Most runners do this by starting with a combination of jogging and walking. They gradually increase to running more and walking less. Before you know it, you will be running all the time!

During your first couple of weeks, try running for one minute without stopping, followed immediately by walking for two minutes, and then running for another minute. If that's too easy for you, try two minutes of running followed by two minutes of walking. However, if one minute is tough for you, don't worry. Keep running for a minute at a time until it feels easier.

After a difficult run, it can be hard to get out the door for your next run. Setting goals is one way to keep your motivation up. Set a couple of realistic goals for the length of your run before you start. Make up your mind to reach these goals.

Many runners make training plans to help them reach their goals. To make one, chart out on a calendar how you will increase your running during a training period: a week, a month, or several months. A training plan helps you map out the steps you need to take to reach your goals.

Going Full Speed

Do you like to run as fast as your legs will carry you? If so, sprinting might be for you.

A sprint is a short footrace. Official sprint distances include the 55-, 100-, and 200-meter dashes. Because the races are short, a sprinter tries to reach full speed as quickly as possible.

A sprinter needs arm, leg, and core strength, coordination, and speed. To develop these skills, sprinters do technique drills and strength training in addition to running. Sprinters use starting blocks, and they practice their starts regularly during

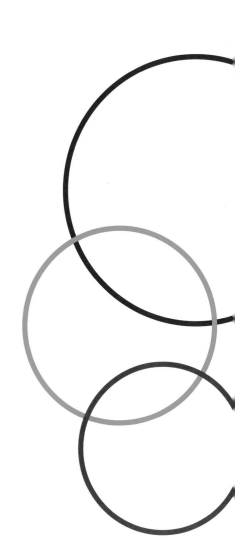

training. Sprinters don't run as far during training as athletes preparing for longer races. But because sprinters run faster during training, they need more time to recover between sprints.

Pace Yourself

If you like a long, paced run, you may want to try distance running.

Unlike sprints, distance running requires you to pace yourself. The longer a run, the more patient a runner must be. When the body becomes tired, its natural instinct is to stop. Distance runners keep going and are often surprised by what they can accomplish when they try. Distance running takes place on tracks, roads, and cross-country courses.

A typical week of training for a distance runner will include a variety of steady runs, faster running, and one longer run. This long run is one of the most important parts of training for a distance runner. During a long run, a distance runner runs at a slow, even pace. If you want to try this, you should start at a relatively short distance, such as 1 to 3 miles (1.6 to 4.8 km), and slowly add ½ mile (0.8 km) per week.

Many distance runners do some speed workouts. Once you can run 15 minutes without stopping, you might want to try a *fartlek*, a workout with fast and slow running. In Swedish, fartlek means "speed play." During a run, pick up your pace for 30 seconds to two minutes, and then resume your original speed. When you run faster, don't go at full speed. You don't want to be too tired to finish the rest of your run. As you become a more experienced runner, you can increase the length and speed of these pickups.

Running Form

Because running is a basic skill for people, it might be hard to imagine that you can spend a lot of time improving your running skills or technique. This is a common myth about running. No matter what distance you decide to run, running form, or the combination of running posture and movement, affects your performance.

When you run, you need to have good posture. What does good posture look like when you are running? It doesn't look much different from when you are standing with good posture. You should stand with a straight back and your head level. Your face should be relaxed, and your eyes should focus a few feet in front of you. Your torso, or center, should be in line with your head and hips.

Your core refers to the area above the center of your pelvis. Your core keeps you upright, and running works this area of your body. Your core should not be behind or in front of the rest of your body. Some runners make the mistake of "sitting down," so that their legs are in front—instead of straight under their core—as they run.

Your hands should be gently cupped, not tightly clenched or floppy. Some runners prefer to run with their palms open, facing their bodies, and their fingers touching one another. With your shoulders relaxed, your arms should swing in a back-and-forth motion. Your elbows should be bent and kept close to your sides.

Hitting Your Stride

Something as simple as running is actually many movements working together. These movements are called the stride cycle.

If your first step is with your right foot, your left knee bends underneath your body. After landing, your right foot pushes off, driving your body forward. As your left leg reaches forward to make contact with the ground and become the driving leg, your right foot trails behind your body. During this phase of the stride cycle, for a brief moment, the body is not supported by either foot. Your left leg extends in front of your body, then your foot makes contact with the ground and pushes off. Your left leg follows through, trailing behind your body, while your right knee bends and comes forward and your right foot prepares to strike the ground. All the while, each arm moves forward with the opposite leg to help you keep your balance. The cycle repeats.

Your foot should hit the ground when your body is directly above your foot. Most people land on their midfoot, the area just behind the ball, or front, of the foot. This allows the runner's body to continue to propel itself forward smoothly.

Practice Makes Perfect

Technique drills, also called sprint drills, help develop good running form. Think of these drills as the secret to making running easier and more fun. When you do these regularly, once or twice a week, your muscles will grow stronger and help you during your runs.

Technique drills break down running into separate exercises that exaggerate the various parts of the running cycle.

High knees: Run in place or run slowly across a short distance, 50 meters or less, and bring your knees higher than normal toward your waist. Vigorously swing your arms. Your hands should come up higher than usual, but not above your shoulders.

Bounding for height: A bounding step is a one-footed leap. Begin by pushing off your planted foot—the foot that is on the ground—to achieve more height. Your opposite knee should bend and come up as high as possible. Use the arm opposite your bending leg to drive your body upward. Your elbows should be bent loosely, and your hands should go as high as your head.

Bounding for distance: Instead of bounding for height, push farther forward with your planted foot. Your opposite leg should bend slightly, and your arms should remain loose. Use the momentum from your arm swing to drive you forward.

Accelerations: Run at a slow, relaxed pace. Pick up speed for about 15 to 20 meters, and then slowly ease out of the sprint. After each sprint, take a break, walking the same distance that you ran.

Preventing Injuries

Warm up your muscles by jogging at an easy pace. Warming up is a fun way to ease into your training runs and workouts. It allows your muscles to lengthen. These long, warm muscles are less likely to get strained or pulled than a short, "cold" muscle is. Walking and biking are also good warm-up activities.

Stretching also helps prevent injuries. Being flexible is one of the best ways to maximize your training, efficiency, and talent. The best time to stretch is

between your warm up and your run. You should also stretch after your training run, workout, or race. Although you will be tired, these post-run stretches lengthen your muscles and increase your flexibility.

After a run, you will likely be tired and may not feel like running again, but easing out of a run with a cooldown, or a slow jog or brisk walk, helps your body recover more quickly.

Recovery between training runs is important, too. After all that work, be sure to get a good night's sleep. When you are training, some of your muscle cells get damaged. As these cells are repaired, your muscles build and get stronger. To help your body with this process, get plenty of rest and eat a balanced diet.

Keeping Track

A training log is a notebook in which a runner keeps track of all training, goals, and races. You can use a training log to look back and see how hard you have worked. You can add up how far you have run or how many workouts you have finished. It's not easy remembering what you did during every training session unless you write it down each time. If you find yourself unmotivated or injured, a training log will give you a description of what you have been doing. Use this as a starting point for figuring out how to adjust your training.

Here are items to include in your training log:

- The date and time of your run, workout, or race

- The type of training (easy run, workout, race, strength training, technique drills)

- A description of your workout, if you did one

- How many miles the run or workout was

- How it felt and the level of difficulty

- The location of the run or workout

- What the weather was like and if it affected your training

- A section for comments on rest and nutrition

- A section for races and goals

To the Races!

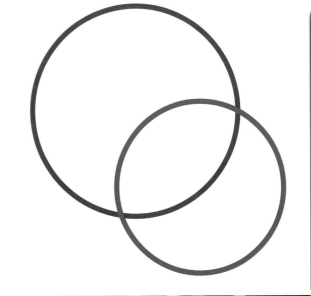

After training so hard, you might want to try a race.

Track-and-field and cross-country competitions are called meets. Each meet is made up of several events. Road races are separate events.

Competition is exciting. With people watching, you might feel your heart race a little before

you even start running. Pre-race nerves are normal, and even the best runners in the world experience this mix of nervousness and excitement.

Creating a routine for meets and races is a good way to deal with jitters. You will want to warm up, stretch, do some technique drills, possibly change into racing spikes or flats, and, if necessary, check in with the race officials before you head to the starting line. If you are on a team, you might do this routine with your teammates.

Even though you are competing against others, you should also try to set a personal best, which is your best time for that distance. This allows you to see how you have improved.

Off and Running

Sprints usually take place on a track, and most sprinters use starting blocks. Starting blocks help runners build speed more quickly. Runners usually stay in one lane on the track, and the finishes can be very close.

Distance runners start standing up. A distance runner leans forward on one foot, which is placed just behind the starting line. The opposite arm is bent and forward as well. The foot farther away from the starting line will be the first to step forward, and the opposite arm will drive the body forward, too. In distance races, the runners usually start standing

next to one another on the starting line. During the first part of the race, runners are allowed to cut to the inside lane and pass runners in the outside lanes as needed.

In a cross-country race, runners start just as they would in a distance race, but the races can include many more people. Runners share lanes, and the starting line can be crowded. The finish line can be just as crowded, depending on the race.

In all races, a close finish is determined by which runner's torso crosses the finish line first. The head, neck, arms, and legs do not count. For this reason, you will often see runners lean with their chests forward at the end of a race.

Time for Teamwork!

Relays are team-based races. Unlike individual races, a relay usually consists of a team of four people who compete against other teams in one race.

In a four-person relay, each runner runs one of four segments of the relay and then hands off a baton to the next runner on the team. In track relays, these handoffs are important because if the baton is dropped, that team can be disqualified. Smooth handoffs are most vital in sprinting races, such as the 400-meter relay. Because the finishes can be so close, any time lost on a bobbled handoff can cost a team the race.

While road relays and cross-country relays do take place, track relays are the most common. Track-relay distances are usually 400 meters, 800 meters, 1,600 meters, or 3,200 meters.

Stars of the Sport

Despite many challenges, Gail Devers makes running fast look easy. She has been at the top of U.S. sprinting lists for about 20 years. Devers battles with Graves' disease, a disorder in which a person's immune system mistakenly attacks the thyroid gland. The disease can lead to a variety of serious health problems, including affecting the person's eyes and skin and causing an irregular heartbeat. But Devers didn't let the disease stop her. At the 1992 Barcelona Olympics, she emerged as the gold medalist in the 100 meters.

She has won several medals at the World Championships. In 1996, she won more Olympic gold medals in the 100-meter dash and in the 400-meter relay. In 2006, at the age of 40, Devers continued to compete at the national and world level.

Jesse Owens was one of the greatest sprinters in U.S. history. As an African-American athlete in the 1930s, he was not treated the same as his fellow athletes. But at the 1936 Berlin Olympics, which took place in Nazi Germany, Owens proved to everyone, including Adolf Hitler, that he was the best sprinter in the world. Owens won the 100-meter dash, 200-meter dash, and broad jump, and was a member of the gold-medal 400-meter relay team.

Speed Demons

On May 6, 1954, Englishman Roger Bannister became the first man to run a mile in less than four minutes. He did it in 3 minutes, 59 seconds. Until Bannister's accomplishment, some believed a runner who ran so far so fast would die. He proved them wrong.

At 16 years old, Grete Waitz became Norway's junior champion in the 400 meters and 800 meters. Two years later, in 1972, she was the national champion in the 800 meters and 1,500 meters. That same year, she went to the Munich Olympics in the 1,500 meters and

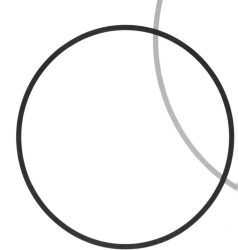

eventually set the world record in the 3,000 meters. But Waitz is best known for her accomplishments as a marathon runner. She ran her first marathon in New York City in 1978. Not only did she win the race, she did it in 2 hours, 32 minutes, 30 seconds, crushing the old world record by about two minutes! At the same marathon the next year, she became the first woman to break the 2:30 mark with a time of 2:27:33. She won nine of 11 New York City marathons during the 1970s and 1980s and in 1984 won the silver medal in the 26.2-mile (42-km) Olympic event.

What Happened When?

776 B.C. **1870** **1880** **1890** **1900** **1910** **1920**

776 B.C. The ancient Olympic Games begin with one event—a short sprint of about 600 feet (183 m).

1876 The English national cross-country championship is founded.

1896 The first Olympic marathon is run at the Athens Olympic Games from the town of Marathon to the Olympic Stadium in Athens, a distance of 26.2 miles (42 km).

1880 Cross-country running is introduced in the United States by the Amateur Athletic Association and Harvard University.

1897 The first Boston Marathon takes place on April 19.

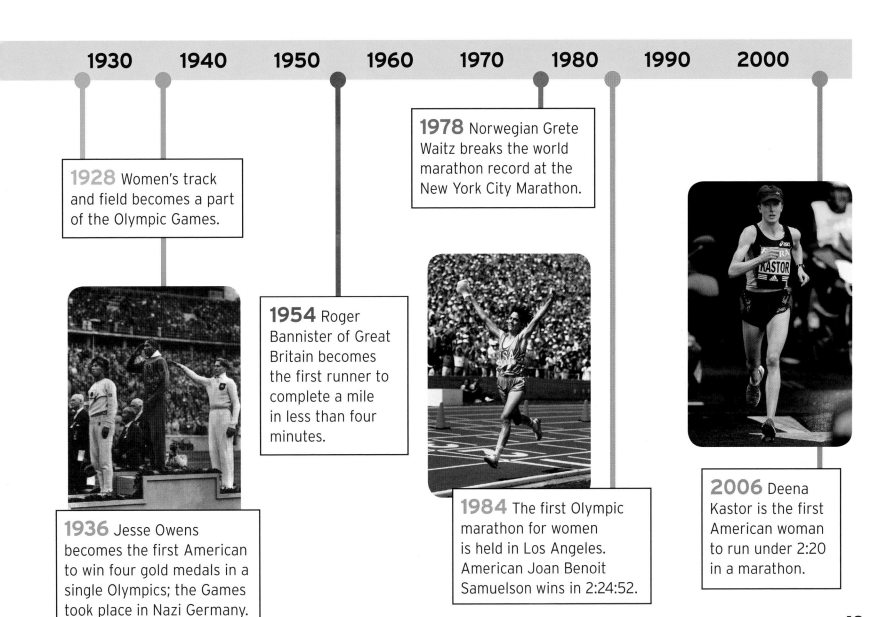

1930　**1940**　**1950**　**1960**　**1970**　**1980**　**1990**　**2000**

1928 Women's track and field becomes a part of the Olympic Games.

1954 Roger Bannister of Great Britain becomes the first runner to complete a mile in less than four minutes.

1978 Norwegian Grete Waitz breaks the world marathon record at the New York City Marathon.

1936 Jesse Owens becomes the first American to win four gold medals in a single Olympics; the Games took place in Nazi Germany.

1984 The first Olympic marathon for women is held in Los Angeles. American Joan Benoit Samuelson wins in 2:24:52.

2006 Deena Kastor is the first American woman to run under 2:20 in a marathon.

Fun Running Facts

In 1960, Ethiopian Abebe Bikila won the Olympic marathon in Rome. In only his second marathon, he ran the race barefoot and broke the world record in a time of 2:15:16.

The New York City Marathon is the biggest marathon in the world, with about 38,000 runners.

The Atlanta Peachtree Road Race is the largest 10K in the world, with 55,000 participants, 3,000 volunteers, and more than 600 portable toilets.

Runners race for fun and for charity. In its quest to cure breast cancer, the annual Susan G. Komen Race for the Cure has drawn millions of participants running 5K races throughout the United States.

In 1884, George Littlewood ran 623.75 miles (1,003.6 km) in six days in Madison Square Garden at an indoor championship "pedestrian race."

Running for fitness was first popularized in the 1960s with the publication of *Distance Running News*. This magazine became *Runner's World* in 1970 and is still the most popular running magazine.

Running Words to Know

accelerations: short sprints in which a runner starts slowly and increases his speed until he is sprinting

baton: hollow tube-shaped stick carried by and exchanged between relay participants

chronograph: special running watch that has a timing function allowing a runner to keep track of how long he or she has been running

cooldown: a short, easy jog after a training run, workout, or race

easy run: a slow recovery run

fartlek: workout that alternates between fast and slow running

hand off: passing the baton from one relay participant to another

long run: the longest run during a training week

marathon: a race that is 26.2 miles (42 km) long

meets: track-and-field or cross-country competitions

pace: measure of the speed of running in minutes per mile or minutes per kilometer

personal best: an individual runner's best time at a certain distance

recovery: time of rest between training sessions; easy runs between harder workouts; or the rest interval in interval training

running form: overall running posture and stride

strength training: weightlifting or resistance training

technique drills: series of skips and hops and leg-and-foot movements practiced to improve a person's running form

training log: record of training over a period of time

warm-up: a short, easy jog or other exercise to loosen muscles before a training run, workout, or race

Other Words to Know

accelerate: to increase speed

core: area of the body above the center of the pelvis

immune system: system that protects the body from infection and disease

irregular: uneven

terrain: ground or land

thyroid gland: gland at the base of a person's neck

torso: part of the body between the neck and waist

traction: gripping power that keeps a person from slipping

Where to Learn More

MORE BOOKS TO READ

Knotts, Bob. *Track and Field*. New York: Children's Press, 2000.

Marsden, Carolyn. *Moon Runner*. Cambridge, Mass.: Candlewick Press, 2005.

Wallace, Rich. *Fast Company*. New York: Viking, 2005.

ON THE ROAD

New York Road Runners Foundation
845 Third Avenue, 11th Floor
New York, NY 10022
212/423-2227

PSA Youth Running Club
c/o Pace Setter Athletic
4306 SE Woodstock Blvd.
Portland, OR 97206
503/777-3214

ON THE WEB

For more information on this topic, use FactHound.

1. Go to *www.facthound.com*
2. Type in this book ID: 0756536294
3. Click on the *Fetch It* button.

FactHound will find the best Web sites for you.

INDEX

ABOUT THE AUTHOR

Jessica Deutsch has been running since she was in the seventh grade. She ran sprint races through high school before becoming a mid- and long-distance runner in college. She runs with the Mississippi River Road Runners, an all-women's club team. Her favorite race is the half-marathon. An avid reader, Deutsch works in publishing and lives in Minneapolis, Minnesota.